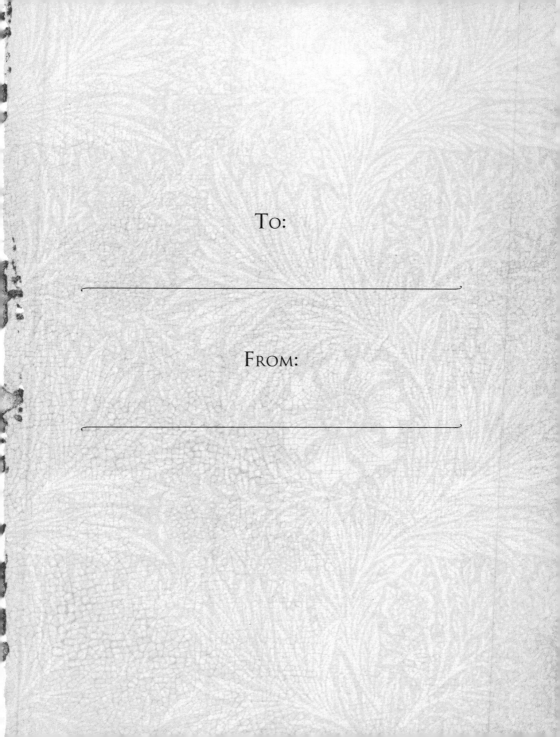

To:

From:

When God Thinks of You...He Smiles

© 2009 Lake House Gifts
A Division of Ellie Claire Gift & Paper Corp.
www.ellieclaire.com

Compiled by Joanie Garborg
Designed by Mick Thurber

Scripture references are from the following sources: The Holy Bible, King James Version (KJV). The Holy
Bible, New International Version (NIV). Copyright © 1973, 1978, 1984 International Bible Society. Used
by permission of Zondervan Bible Publishers. The New American Standard Bible® (NASB), Copyright
© 1960, 1962, 1963, 1968, 1971, 1972, 1973, 1975, 1977, 1995 by The Lockman Foundation. Used
by permission. The Holy Bible, New Living Translation (NLT), copyright 1996. Used by permission
of Tyndale House Publishers, Inc., Wheaton, Illinois 60189. All rights reserved. The Message (MSG).
Copyright © 1994, 1994, 1995, 1996, 2000, 2001, 2002. Used by permission of NavPress Publishing
Group. The New Revised Standard Version Bible: Anglicized Edition (NRSV), copyright 1989, 1995,
Division of Christian Education of the National Council of the Churches of Christ in the United States of
America. Used by permission. All rights reserved. The Living Bible (TLB) © 1971. Used by permission of
Tyndale House Publishers, Inc., Wheaton, Illinois 60189. All rights reserved.

Excluding Scripture verses, references to men and masculine pronouns have been
replaced with gender-neutral references.

ISBN 978-1-935416-44-9

Printed in China

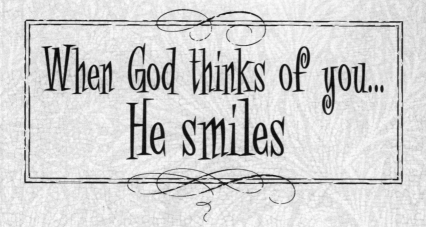

When God thinks of you...
He smiles

PROMISE JOURNAL

LAKE HOUSE
GIFTS

SPECIAL PLANS

This is the real gift: you have been given the breath of life, designed with a unique, one-of-a-kind soul that exists forever—the way that you choose to live it doesn't change the fact that you've been given the gift of being now and forever. Priceless in value, you are handcrafted by God, who has a personal design and plan for each of us.

May God's love guide you through the special plans He has for your life.

Allow your dreams a place in your prayers and plans. God-given dreams can help you move into the future He is preparing for you.

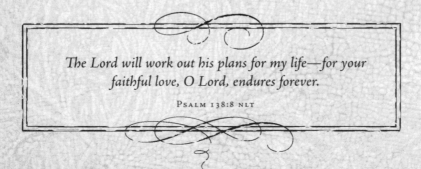

The Lord will work out his plans for my life—for your faithful love, O Lord, endures forever.

PSALM 138:8 NLT

SPECIAL PLANS

....
....
....
....
....
....
....
....
....
....
....
....
....
....
....
....
....

WONDERFUL LOVE

Show the wonder of your great love…. Keep me as the apple of your eye;
hide me in the shadow of your wings.

PSALM 17:7–8 NIV

Give thanks to the Lord, for he is good! His faithful love endures forever.

PSALM 136:1 NLT

The Lord is gracious and merciful, slow to anger and abounding in steadfast
love. The Lord is good to all, and his compassion is over all that he has made.
The Lord is faithful in all his words, and gracious in all his deeds.

PSALM 145:8-9, 13 NRSV

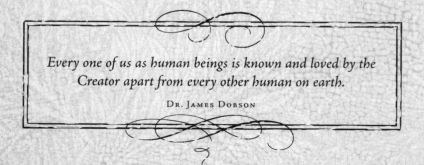

*Every one of us as human beings is known and loved by the
Creator apart from every other human on earth.*

DR. JAMES DOBSON

WONDERFUL LOVE

COUNTLESS BEAUTIES

May God give you eyes to see beauty only the heart can understand.

From the world we see, hear, and touch, we behold inspired visions that reveal God's glory. In the sun's light, we catch warm rays of grace and glimpse His eternal design. In the birds' song, we hear His voice and it reawakens our desire for Him. At the wind's touch, we feel His Spirit and sense our eternal existence.

All the world is an utterance of the Almighty. Its countless beauties, its exquisite adaptations, all speak to you of Him.

PHILLIPS BROOKS

Worship the Lord in the beauty of holiness.

PSALM 96:9 NIV

COUNTLESS BEAUTIES

THE GRACE OF GOD

But God, being rich in mercy, because of His great love with which He loved us, even when we were dead in our transgressions, made us alive together with Christ (by grace you have been saved), and raised us up with Him, and seated us with Him in the heavenly places in Christ Jesus, so that in the ages to come He might show the surpassing riches of His grace in kindness toward us in Christ Jesus. For by grace you have been saved through faith; and that not of yourselves, it is the gift of God; not as a result of works, so that no one may boast. For we are His workmanship, created in Christ Jesus for good works, which God prepared beforehand so that we would walk in them.

EPHESIANS 2:4–10 NASB

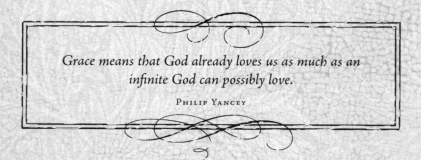

Grace means that God already loves us as much as an infinite God can possibly love.

PHILIP YANCEY

THE GRACE OF GOD

....

....

....

....

....

....

....

....

....

....

....

....

....

....

....

....

....

....

....

HOLD FAST YOUR DREAMS

Hold fast your dreams!

Within your heart

Keep one still, secret spot

Where dreams may go

And, sheltered so,

May thrive and grow…

O keep a place apart,

Within your heart,

For little dreams to go!

LOUISE DRISCOLL

Always stay connected to people and seek out things that bring you joy.

Dream with abandon. Pray confidently.

BARBARA JOHNSON

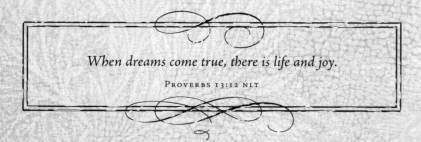

When dreams come true, there is life and joy.

PROVERBS 13:12 NLT

HOLD FAST YOUR DREAMS

GOD-PROVISION

Steep yourself in God-reality, God-initiative, God-provisions. You'll find all your everyday human concerns will be met. Don't be afraid of missing out. You're my dearest friends! The Father wants to give you the very kingdom itself.

LUKE 12:28 MSG

Your Father knows that you need these things. But seek His kingdom, and these things will be added to you. Do not be afraid, little flock, for your Father has chosen gladly to give you the kingdom.

LUKE 12:30–31 NASB

I am like a luxuriant fruit tree. Everything you need is to be found in me.

HOSEA 14:8 MSG

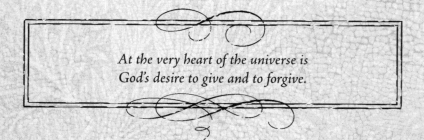

*At the very heart of the universe is
God's desire to give and to forgive.*

GOD-PROVISION

THE GOODNESS OF GOD

The goodness of God is infinitely more wonderful than we will ever be able to comprehend.

A. W. TOZER

All that is good, all that is true, all that is beautiful, all that is beneficent, be it great or small, be it perfect or fragmentary, natural as well as supernatural, moral as well as material, comes from God.

CARDINAL JOHN HENRY NEWMAN

We walk without fear, full of hope and courage and strength to do His will, waiting for the endless good which He is always giving as fast as He can get us able to take it in.

GEORGE MACDONALD

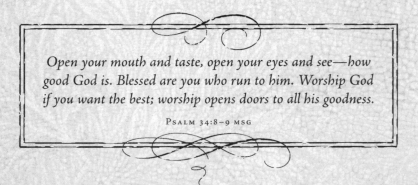

Open your mouth and taste, open your eyes and see—how good God is. Blessed are you who run to him. Worship God if you want the best; worship opens doors to all his goodness.

PSALM 34:8–9 MSG

THE GOODNESS OF GOD

....

....

....

....

....

....

....

....

....

....

....

....

....

....

THE MAJESTY OF GOD

O Lord, our Lord, how majestic is your name in all the earth! You have set your glory above the heavens…. When I consider your heavens, the work of your fingers, the moon and the stars, which you have set in place, what is man that you are mindful of him, the son of man that you care for him? You made him a little lower than the heavenly beings and crowned him with glory and honor. O Lord, our Lord, how majestic is your name in all the earth!

PSALM 8:1–5, 9 NIV

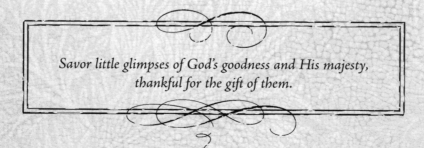

Savor little glimpses of God's goodness and His majesty,
thankful for the gift of them.

THE MAJESTY OF GOD

CHILD OF GOD

When we call on God, He bends down His ear to listen, as a father bends down to listen to his little child.

ELIZABETH CHARLES

He only is the Maker
of all things near and far;
He paints the wayside flower,
He lights the evening star;
the wind and waves obey Him,
by Him the birds are fed;
much more to us, His children,
He gives our daily bread.

MATTHIAS CLAUDIUS

Remember you are very special to God as His precious child. He has promised to complete the good work He has begun in you. As you continue to grow in Him, He will make you a blessing to others.

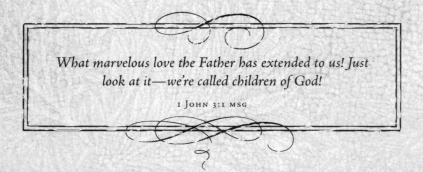

What marvelous love the Father has extended to us! Just look at it—we're called children of God!

1 JOHN 3:1 MSG

CHILD OF GOD

THE BLESSING OF THE LORD

The Lord bless thee, and keep thee: the Lord make his face shine upon thee, and be gracious unto thee: the Lord lift up his countenance upon thee, and give thee peace.

NUMBERS 6:24–26 KJV

May the favor of the Lord our God rest upon us;

establish the work of our hands for us—

yes, establish the work of our hands.

PSALM 90:17 NIV

How blessed is everyone who fears the Lord, who walks in His ways.

PSALM 128:1 NASB

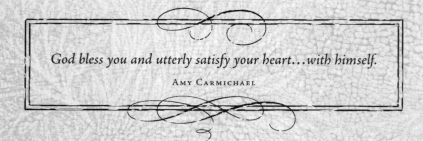

God bless you and utterly satisfy your heart…with himself.

AMY CARMICHAEL

THE BLESSING OF THE LORD

....

....

....

....

....

....

....

....

....

....

....

....

....

....

....

....

....

....

SPECIAL GIFTS

Every person ever created is so special that their presence in the world makes it richer and fuller and more wonderful than it could ever have been without them.

We were not sent into this world to do anything into which we cannot put our hearts.

JOHN RUSKIN

Use what talents you possess: the woods would be very silent if no birds sang there except those that sang best.

HENRY VAN DYKE

God gives everyone a special gift and a special place to use it.

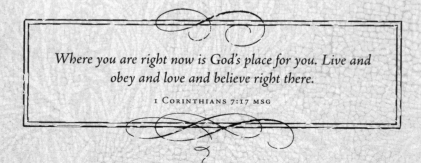

Where you are right now is God's place for you. Live and obey and love and believe right there.

1 CORINTHIANS 7:17 MSG

SPECIAL GIFTS

LOVE ONE ANOTHER

Watch what God does, and then you do it, like children who learn proper behavior from their parents. Mostly what God does is love you. Keep company with him and learn a life of love. Observe how Christ loved us. His love was not cautious but extravagant. He didn't love in order to get something from us but to give everything of himself to us. Love like that.

EPHESIANS 5:1–2 MSG

I pray that your love for each other will overflow more and more, and that you will keep on growing in your knowledge and understanding.

PHILIPPIANS 1:9 NLT

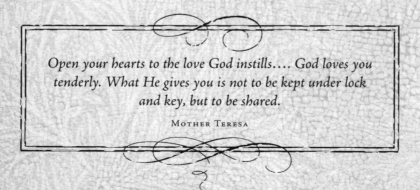

Open your hearts to the love God instills.... God loves you tenderly. What He gives you is not to be kept under lock and key, but to be shared.

MOTHER TERESA

LOVE ONE ANOTHER

In His Image

God's designs regarding you, and His methods of bringing about these designs, are infinitely wise.

MADAME JEANNE GUYON

Stand outside this evening. Look at the stars. Know that you are special and loved by the One who created them.

All that we have and are is one of the unique and never-to-be repeated ways God has chosen to express himself in space and time. Each of us, made in His image and likeness, is yet another promise He has made to the universe that He will continue to love it and care for it.

BRENNAN MANNING

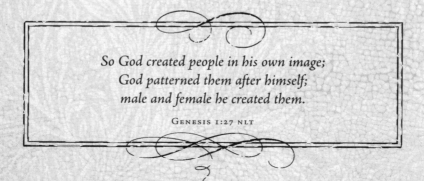

So God created people in his own image;
God patterned them after himself;
male and female he created them.

GENESIS 1:27 NLT

IN HIS IMAGE

WONDERFUL JOY

So be truly glad! There is wonderful joy ahead. You love him even though you have never seen him. Though you do not see him, you trust him; and even now you are happy with a glorious, inexpressible joy.

1 Peter 1:6, 8–9 nlt

And the ransomed of the Lord will return. They will enter Zion with singing; everlasting joy will crown their heads. Gladness and joy will overtake them, and sorrow and sighing will flee away.

Isaiah 35:10 niv

Rejoice evermore.

1 Thessalonians 5:16 kjv

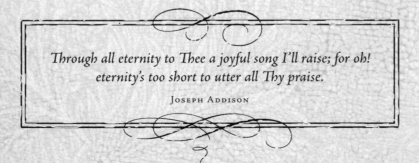

Through all eternity to Thee a joyful song I'll raise; for oh! eternity's too short to utter all Thy praise.

Joseph Addison

WONDERFUL JOY

A LIFE TRANSFORMED

To pray is to change. This is a great grace. How good of God to provide a path whereby our lives can be taken over by love and joy and peace and patience and kindness and goodness and faithfulness and gentleness and self-control.

RICHARD J. FOSTER

For God is, indeed, a wonderful Father who longs to pour out His mercy upon us, and whose majesty is so great that He can transform us from deep within.

TERESA OF AVILA

A life transformed by the power of God is always a marvel and a miracle.

GERALDINE NICHOLAS

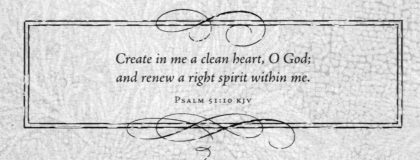

Create in me a clean heart, O God;
and renew a right spirit within me.

PSALM 51:10 KJV

A LIFE TRANSFORMED

GOD'S CARE

The Lord is my shepherd; I shall not want. He maketh me to lie down in green pastures: he leadeth me beside the still waters. He restoreth my soul: he leadeth me in the paths of righteousness for his name's sake. Yea, though I walk through the valley of the shadow of death, I will fear no evil: for thou art with me; thy rod and thy staff they comfort me. Thou preparest a table before me in the presence of mine enemies: thou anointest my head with oil; my cup runneth over. Surely goodness and mercy shall follow me all the days of my life: and I will dwell in the house of the Lord for ever.

PSALM 23:1–6 KJV

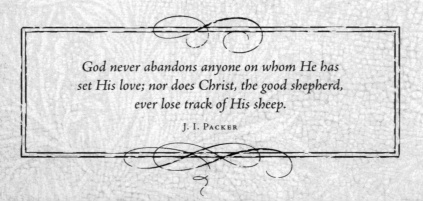

God never abandons anyone on whom He has set His love; nor does Christ, the good shepherd, ever lose track of His sheep.

J. I. PACKER

GOD'S CARE

A WORK OF ART

Each one of us is God's special work of art. Through us, He teaches and inspires, delights and encourages, informs and uplifts all those who view our lives. God, the master artist, is most concerned about expressing himself—His thoughts and His intentions—through what He paints in our character.… [He] wants to paint a beautiful portrait of His Son in and through your life. A painting like no other in all of time.

JONI EARECKSON TADA

Whether we are poets or parents or teachers or artists or gardeners, we must start where we are and use what we have. In the process of creation and relationship, what seems mundane and trivial may show itself to be holy, precious, part of a pattern.

LUCI SHAW

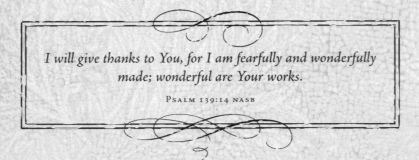

I will give thanks to You, for I am fearfully and wonderfully made; wonderful are Your works.

PSALM 139:14 NASB

A WORK OF ART

GOD'S WAYS

O the depth of the riches both of the wisdom and knowledge of God! How unsearchable are his judgments, and his ways past finding out! For who hath known the mind of the Lord? or who hath been his counsellor?

ROMANS 11:33–34 KJV

For my thoughts are not your thoughts, neither are your ways my ways, saith the Lord. For as the heavens are higher than the earth, so are my ways higher than your ways, and my thoughts than your thoughts.

ISAIAH 55:8–9 KJV

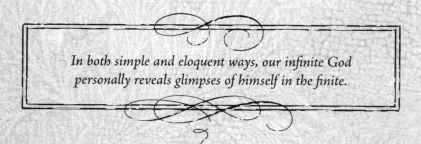

In both simple and eloquent ways, our infinite God personally reveals glimpses of himself in the finite.

GOD'S WAYS

ENFOLDED IN PEACE

I will let God's peace infuse every part of today. As the chaos swirls and life's demands pull at me on all sides, I will breathe in God's peace that surpasses all understanding. He has promised that He would set within me a peace too deeply planted to be affected by unexpected or exhausting demands.

Calm me, O Lord, as you stilled the storm,
Still me, O Lord, keep me from harm.
Let all the tumult within me cease,
Enfold me, Lord, in your peace.

CELTIC TRADITIONAL

God cannot give us a happiness and peace apart from himself, because it is not there. There is no such thing.

C. S. LEWIS

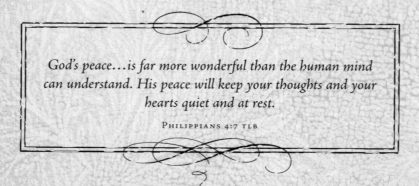

God's peace…is far more wonderful than the human mind can understand. His peace will keep your thoughts and your hearts quiet and at rest.

PHILIPPIANS 4:7 TLB

ENFOLDED IN PEACE

RESTORATION

The Spirit of the Sovereign Lord is on me, because the Lord has anointed me to preach good news to the poor. He has sent me to bind up the brokenhearted, to proclaim freedom for the captives and release from darkness for the prisoners, to proclaim the year of the Lord's favor and the day of vengeance of our God, to comfort all who mourn, and provide for those who grieve in Zion—to bestow on them a crown of beauty instead of ashes, the oil of gladness instead of mourning, and a garment of praise instead of a spirit of despair. They will be called oaks of righteousness, a planting of the Lord for the display of his splendor.

ISAIAH 61:1–3 NIV

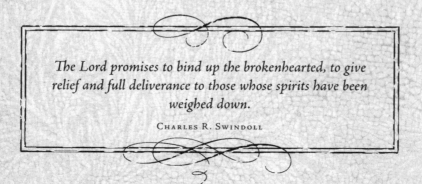

The Lord promises to bind up the brokenhearted, to give relief and full deliverance to those whose spirits have been weighed down.

CHARLES R. SWINDOLL

RESTORATION

A SPLENDID GIFT

This bright, new day, complete with twenty-four hours of opportunities, choices, and attitudes comes with a perfectly matched set of 1440 minutes. This unique gift, this one day, cannot be exchanged, replaced or refunded. Handle with care. Make the most of it. There is only one to a customer!

You have a unique message to deliver, a unique song to sing, a unique act of love to bestow. This message, this song, and this act of love have been entrusted exclusively to the one and only you.

JOHN POWELL, S.J.

Live your life while you have it. Life is a splendid gift—there is nothing small about it.

FLORENCE NIGHTINGALE

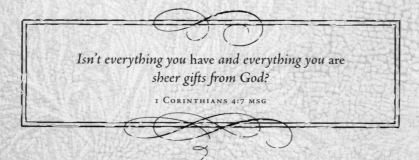

Isn't everything you have *and everything you* are *sheer gifts from God?*

1 CORINTHIANS 4:7 MSG

A SPLENDID GIFT

DESIGNED ON PURPOSE

It's in Christ that we find out who we are and what we are living for.
Long before we first heard of Christ and got our hopes up, he had his
eye on us, had designs on us for glorious living, part of the overall purpose
he is working out in everything and everyone.

EPHESIANS 1:11–12 MSG

To every thing there is a season, and a time to every purpose under the
heaven.

ECCLESIASTES 3:1 KJV

All the days ordained for me were written in your book before one of
them came to be.

PSALM 139:15-16 NIV

I delight to do thy will, O my God.

PSALM 40:8 KJV

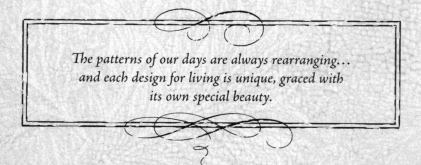

The patterns of our days are always rearranging…
and each design for living is unique, graced with
its own special beauty.

DESIGNED ON PURPOSE

GOD HEARS

No matter where we are, God can hear us from there!

And then a little laughing prayer
Came running up the sky,
Above the golden gutters, where
The sorry prayers go by.
It had no fear of anything,
But in that holy place
It found the very throne of God
And smiled up in His face.

AMY CARMICHAEL

*We can now come fearlessly into God's presence,
assured of his glad welcome.*

EPHESIANS 3:12 NLT

G O D   H E A R S

....

....

....

....

....

....

....

....

....

....

....

....

....

....

....

....

SEEK FIRST

Look at the birds of the air, that they do not sow, nor reap nor gather into barns, and yet your heavenly Father feeds them. Are you not worth much more than they? And who of you by being worried can add a single hour to his life? And why are you worried about clothing? Observe how the lilies of the field grow; they do not toil nor do they spin, yet I say to you that not even Solomon in all his glory clothed himself like one of these. But if God so clothes the grass of the field, which is alive today and tomorrow is thrown into the furnace, will He not much more clothe you? You of little faith! Do not worry then, saying, "What will we eat?" or "What will we drink?" or "What will we wear for clothing?" For…your heavenly Father knows that you need all these things. But seek first His kingdom and His righteousness, and all these things will be added to you.

MATTHEW 6:26–33 NASB

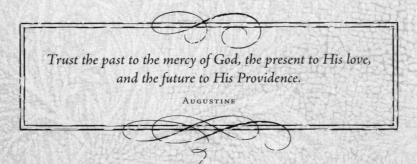

Trust the past to the mercy of God, the present to His love, and the future to His Providence.

AUGUSTINE

SEEK FIRST

....

....

....

....

....

....

....

....

....

....

....

....

....

....

....

....

....

SOUGHT AND FOUND

It is God's will that we believe that we see Him continually, though it seems to us that the sight be only partial; and through this belief He makes us always to gain more grace, for God wishes to be seen, and He wishes to be sought, and He wishes to be expected, and He wishes to be trusted.

JULIAN OF NORWICH

To seek God means first of all to let yourself be found by Him.

God's nature is given me. His love is jealous for my life. All His attributes are woven into the pattern of my spirit. What a God is this! His life implanted in every child. Thank you, Father, for this.

JIM ELLIOT

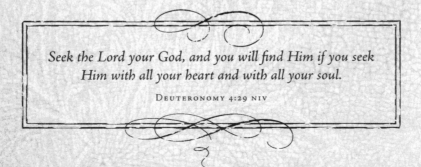

Seek the Lord your God, and you will find Him if you seek Him with all your heart and with all your soul.

DEUTERONOMY 4:29 NIV

SOUGHT AND FOUND

THE PROMISE OF REST

The promise of "arrival" and "rest" is still there for God's people. God himself is at rest. And at the end of the journey we'll surely rest with God. So let's keep at it and eventually arrive at the place of rest.

HEBREWS 4:9–11 MSG

Come unto me, all ye that labour and are heavy laden, and I will give you rest. Take my yoke upon you, and learn of me; for I am meek and lowly in heart: and ye shall find rest unto your souls. For my yoke is easy, and my burden is light.

MATTHEW 11:28–30 KJV

I will refresh the weary and satisfy the faint.

JEREMIAH 31:25 NIV

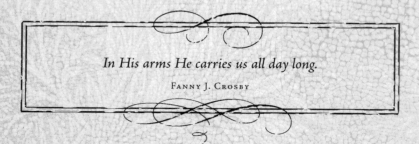

In His arms He carries us all day long.

FANNY J. CROSBY

THE PROMISE OF REST

....
....
....
....
....
....
....
....
....
....
....
....
....
....
....
....
....
....
....
....

THE BEAUTY OF GOD'S PEACE

In comparison with this big world, the human heart is only a small thing. Though the world is so large, it is utterly unable to satisfy this tiny heart. Our ever growing soul and its capacities can be satisfied only in the infinite God. As water is restless until it reaches its level, so the soul has no peace until it rests in God.

SADHU SUNDAR SINGH

Peace is a margin of power around our daily need. Peace is a consciousness of springs too deep for earthly droughts to dry up.

HARRY EMERSON FOSDICK

Drop Thy still dews of quietness

till all our strivings cease;

take from our souls the strain and stress,

and let our ordered lives confess

the beauty of Thy peace.

JOHN GREENLEAF WHITTIER

Be still, and know that I am God.

PSALM 46:10 KJV

THE BEAUTY OF GOD'S PEACE

PROTECTION

The Lord is my light and my salvation—whom shall I fear? The Lord is the stronghold of my life—of whom shall I be afraid? One thing I ask of the Lord, this is what I seek: that I may dwell in the house of the Lord all the days of my life, to gaze upon the beauty of the Lord and to seek him in his temple. For in the day of trouble he will keep me safe in his dwelling; he will hide me in the shelter of his tabernacle and set me high upon a rock. Hear my voice when I call, O Lord; be merciful to me and answer me. My heart says of you, "Seek his face!" Your face, Lord, I will seek.

PSALM 27:1, 4–5, 7–8 NIV

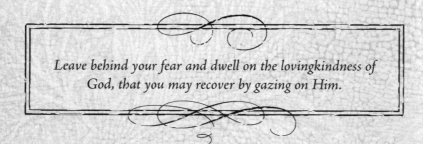

Leave behind your fear and dwell on the lovingkindness of God, that you may recover by gazing on Him.

P R O T E C T I O N

FRESH INSIGHTS

With God, life is eternal—both in quality and length. There is no joy comparable to the joy of discovering something new from God, about God. If the continuing life is a life of joy, we will go on discovering, learning.

EUGENIA PRICE

This life is not all. It is an "unfinished symphony"…with those who know that they are related to God and have felt the power of an endless life.

HENRY WARD BEECHER

Every day we live is a priceless gift of God, loaded with possibilities to learn something new, to gain fresh insights.

DALE EVANS ROGERS

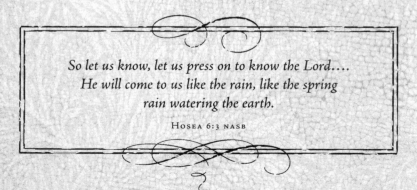

*So let us know, let us press on to know the Lord….
He will come to us like the rain, like the spring
rain watering the earth.*

HOSEA 6:3 NASB

FRESH INSIGHTS

GOOD PLANS

Do not forget the things I have done throughout history. For I am God—
I alone! I am God, and there is no one else like me. Only I can tell you what
is going to happen even before it happens. Everything I plan will come to
pass, for I do whatever I wish.

ISAIAH 46:9–10 NLT

"For I know the plans I have for you," declares the Lord, "plans to prosper
you and not to harm you, plans to give you hope and a future."

JEREMIAH 29:11 NIV

No eye has seen, no ear has heard, no mind has conceived what God has
prepared for those who love him.

1 CORINTHIANS 2:9 NIV

Every person's life is a fairy tale written by God's fingers.

HANS CHRISTIAN ANDERSEN

GOOD PLANS

....
....
....
....
....
....
....
....
....
....
....
....
....
....
....
....
....
....
....

TREASURE IN NATURE

If we are children of God, we have a tremendous treasure in nature and will realize that it is holy and sacred. We will see God reaching out to us in every wind that blows, every sunrise and sunset, every cloud in the sky, every flower that blooms, and every leaf that fades.

OSWALD CHAMBERS

The longer I live, the more my mind dwells upon the beauty and the wonder of the world.

JOHN BURROUGHS

Look up at all the stars in the night sky and hear your Father saying, "I carefully set each one in its place. Know that I love you more than these." Sit by the lake's edge, listening to the water lapping the shore and hear your Father gently calling you to that place near His heart.

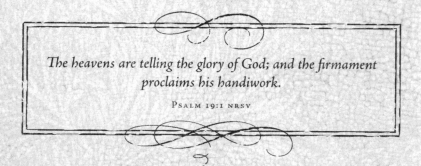

The heavens are telling the glory of God; and the firmament proclaims his handiwork.

PSALM 19:1 NRSV

TREASURE IN NATURE

FEAR NOT

Don't be afraid, I've redeemed you. I've called your name. You're mine.
When you're in over your head, I'll be there with you. When you're in
rough waters, you will not go down. When you're between a rock and
a hard place, it won't be a dead end—because I am God, your personal
God, The Holy of Israel, your Savior. I paid a huge price for you!
That's how much you mean to me! *That's* how much I love you!

ISAIAH 43:1–4 MSG

If God be for us, who can be against us?

ROMANS 8:31 KJV

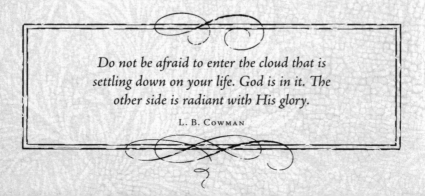

Do not be afraid to enter the cloud that is
settling down on your life. God is in it. The
other side is radiant with His glory.

L. B. COWMAN

FEAR NOT

....

....

....

....

....

....

....

....

....

....

....

....

....

....

....

....

COMPLETELY LOVED

What good news! God knows me completely and still loves me.

You are valuable just because you exist. Not because of what you do or what you have done, but simply because you are. Just think about the way Jesus honors you…and smile.

MAX LUCADO

We are of such value to God that He came to live among us…and to guide us home. He will go to any length to seek us…. We can only respond by loving God for His love.

CATHERINE OF SIENA

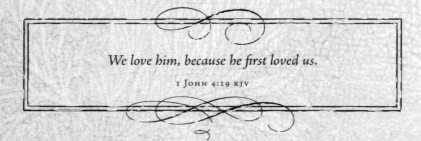

We love him, because he first loved us.

1 JOHN 4:19 KJV

COMPLETELY LOVED

....

....

....

....

....

....

....

....

....

....

....

....

....

....

....

....

....

....

FULL PROTECTION

But let all who take refuge in you be glad; let them ever sing for joy. Spread your protection over them, that those who love your name may rejoice in you. For surely, O Lord, you bless the righteous; you surround them with your favor as with a shield.

PSALM 5:11–12 NIV

I will make my people strong with power from me! They will go wherever they wish, and wherever they go, they will be under my personal care.

ZECHARIAH 10:12 TLB

You have done so much for those who come to you for protection, blessing them before the watching world.

PSALM 31:19 NLT

I am with you and will keep you wherever you go.

GENESIS 28:15 NASB

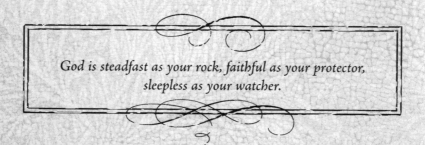

God is steadfast as your rock, faithful as your protector, sleepless as your watcher.

FULL PROTECTION

UNCONDITIONAL LOVE

There is nothing we can do that will make God love us less, and there's nothing we can do that will make Him love us more. He will always and forever love us unconditionally. What He wants from us is that we love Him back with all our heart.

Do not dwell upon your inner failings.... Just do this: Bring your soul to the Great Physician—exactly as you are, even and especially at your worst moment.... For it is in such moments that you will most readily sense His healing presence.

TERESA OF AVILA

If you have a special need today, focus your full attention on the goodness and greatness of your Father rather than on the size of your need. Your need is so small compared to His ability to meet it.

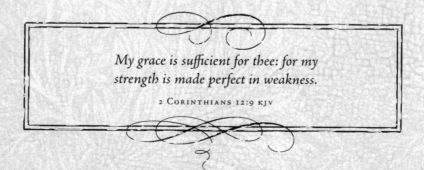

My grace is sufficient for thee: for my strength is made perfect in weakness.

2 CORINTHIANS 12:9 KJV

UNCONDITIONAL LOVE

SHOWERS OF BLESSINGS

Bless the Lord, O my soul: and all that is within me, bless his holy name. Bless the Lord, O my soul, and forget not all his benefits: Who forgiveth all thine iniquities; who healeth all thy diseases; who redeemeth thy life from destruction; who crowneth thee with lovingkindness and tender mercies; who satisfieth thy mouth with good things; so that thy youth is renewed like the eagle's.

PSALM 103:1–5 KJV

I will send showers, showers of blessings, which will come just when they are needed.

EZEKIEL 34:26 NLT

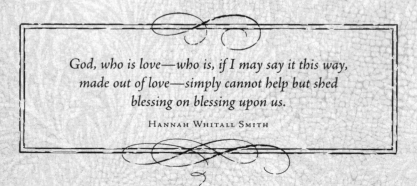

God, who is love—who is, if I may say it this way, made out of love—simply cannot help but shed blessing on blessing upon us.

HANNAH WHITALL SMITH

SHOWERS OF BLESSINGS

ETERNAL HOPE

Hope floods my heart with delight!
Running on air, mad with life, dizzy, reeling,
Upward I mount—faith is sight, life is feeling....
I am immortal! I know it! I feel it!

MARGARET WITTER FULLER

Hope sees the invisible, feels the intangible, and achieves the impossible.

Life is what we are alive to. It is not length but breadth.... Be alive to...
goodness, kindness, purity, love, history, poetry, music, flowers, stars, God,
and eternal hope.

MALTBIE D. BABCOCK

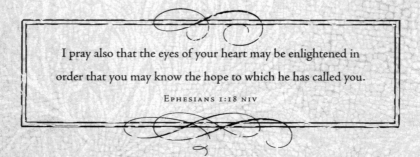

I pray also that the eyes of your heart may be enlightened in
order that you may know the hope to which he has called you.

EPHESIANS 1:18 NIV

ETERNAL HOPE

GOD IS OUR REFUGE

Hear my cry, O God; give heed to my prayer. From the end of the earth
I call to You when my heart is faint; lead me to the rock that is higher
than I. For You have been a refuge for me, a tower of strength against the
enemy. Let me dwell in Your tent forever; let me take refuge in the shelter
of Your wings.

PSALM 61:1–4 NASB

Whom have I in heaven but You? And besides You, I desire nothing on
earth. My flesh and my heart may fail, but God is the strength of my
heart and my portion forever. As for me, the nearness of God is my good;
I have made the Lord God my refuge.

PSALM 73:25–26, 28 NASB

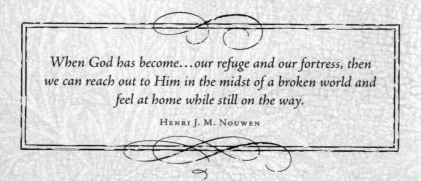

*When God has become…our refuge and our fortress, then
we can reach out to Him in the midst of a broken world and
feel at home while still on the way.*

HENRI J. M. NOUWEN

GOD IS OUR REFUGE

OVERFLOWING PRAISE

All enjoyment spontaneously overflows into praise.... The world rings with praise...walkers praising the countryside, players praising their favorite game.... I think we delight to praise what we enjoy because the praise not merely expresses but completes the enjoyment; it is the appointed consummation.

C. S. LEWIS

God's pursuit of praise from us and our pursuit of pleasure in Him are one and the same pursuit. God's quest to be glorified and our quest to be satisfied reach their goal in this one experience: our delight in God which overflows in praise.

JOHN PIPER

Earth, with her thousand voices, praises God.

SAMUEL TAYLOR COLERIDGE

O sing unto the Lord a new song:
sing unto the Lord, all the earth.

PSALM 96:1 KJV

O V E R F L O W I N G   P R A I S E

LOVE NEVER FAILS

If I speak with the tongues of men and of angels, but do not have love, I have become a noisy gong or a clanging cymbal. If I have the gift of prophecy, and know all mysteries and all knowledge; and if I have all faith, so as to remove mountains, but do not have love, I am nothing. And if I give all my possessions to feed the poor, and if I surrender my body to be burned, but do not have love, it profits me nothing. Love is patient, love is kind and is not jealous; love does not brag and is not arrogant, does not act unbecomingly; it does not seek its own, is not provoked, does not take into account a wrong suffered, does not rejoice in unrighteousness, but rejoices with the truth; bears all things, believes all things, hopes all things, endures all things. Love never fails.

1 CORINTHIANS 13:1–8 NASB

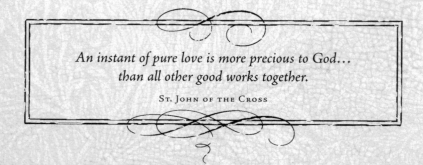

An instant of pure love is more precious to God...
than all other good works together.

ST. JOHN OF THE CROSS

L O V E   N E V E R   F A I L S

A Life of Purpose

Happiness is living by inner purpose, not by outer pressures.

David Augsberger

I believe that nothing that happens to me is meaningless, and that it is good for us all that it should be so, even if it runs counter to our own wishes. As I see it, I'm here for some purpose, and I only hope I may fulfill it.

Dietrich Bonhoeffer

The meaning of earthly existence lies, not as we have grown used to thinking, in prospering, but in the development of the soul.

Aleksandr Solzhenitsyn

And we know that all things work together for good to them that love God, to them who are the called according to his purpose.

Romans 8:28 KJV

A LIFE OF PURPOSE

ABUNDANT LIFE

I came so they can have real and eternal life, more and better life than they
ever dreamed of.

JOHN 10:10 MSG

In the beginning was the Word, and the Word was with God, and the
Word was God. He was in the beginning with God. All things came into
being through Him, and apart from Him nothing came into being that has
come into being. In Him was life, and the life was the Light of men. For of
His fullness we have all received, and grace upon grace.

JOHN 1:1–4, 16 NASB

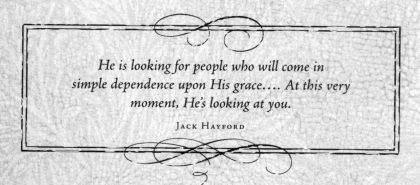

*He is looking for people who will come in
simple dependence upon His grace.... At this very
moment, He's looking at you.*

JACK HAYFORD

ABUNDANT LIFE

His Imprint

The God of the universe—the One who created everything and holds it all in His hand—created each of us in His image, to bear His likeness, His imprint. It is only when Christ dwells within our hearts, radiating the pure light of His love through our humanity that we discover who we are and what we were intended to be.

In the very beginning it was God who formed us by His Word. He made us in His own image. God was spirit and He gave us a spirit so that He could come into us and mingle His own life with our life.

Madame Jeanne Guyon

Made in His image, we can have real meaning, and we can have real knowledge through what He has communicated to us.

Francis Schaeffer

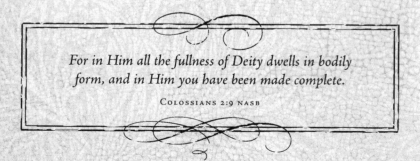

For in Him all the fullness of Deity dwells in bodily form, and in Him you have been made complete.

Colossians 2:9 nasb

HIS IMPRINT

REST IN HIM

My soul finds rest in God alone; my salvation comes from him. He alone is my rock and my salvation; he is my fortress, I will never be shaken. My salvation and my honor depend on God; he is my mighty rock, my refuge. Trust in him at all times, O people; pour out your hearts to him, for God is our refuge. One thing God has spoken, two things have I heard: that you, O God, are strong, and that you, O Lord, are loving.

PSALM 62:1–2, 7–8, 11–12 NIV

Rest in the Lord, and wait patiently for him.

PSALM 37:7 KJV

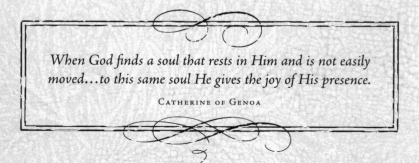

When God finds a soul that rests in Him and is not easily moved…to this same soul He gives the joy of His presence.

CATHERINE OF GENOA

REST IN HIM

HAPPINESS AND GRATITUDE

It is not how much we have, but how much we enjoy, that makes happiness.

CHARLES H. SPURGEON

Sometimes our thoughts turn back toward a corner in a forest, or the end
of a bank, or an orchard powdered with flowers, seen but a single time...
yet remaining in our hearts and leaving in soul and body an unappeased
desire which is not to be forgotten, a feeling we have just rubbed elbows
with happiness.

GUY DE MAUPASSANT

Our inner happiness depends not on what we experience but on the degree
of our gratitude to God, whatever the experience.

ALBERT SCHWEITZER

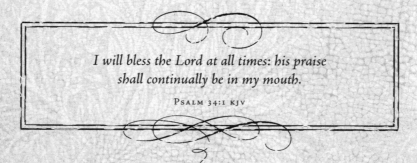

*I will bless the Lord at all times: his praise
shall continually be in my mouth.*

PSALM 34:1 KJV

HAPPINESS AND GRATITUDE

GO OUT IN JOY

You'll go out in joy, you'll be led into a whole and complete life.
The mountains and hills will lead the parade, bursting with song.
All the trees of the forest will join the procession, exuberant with applause.

ISAIAH 55:12 MSG

You have made known to me the path of life; you will fill me with joy in
your presence, with eternal pleasures at your right hand.

PSALM 16:11 NIV

He will yet fill your mouth with laughter and your lips with shouts of joy.

JOB 8:21 NLT

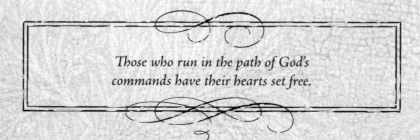

*Those who run in the path of God's
commands have their hearts set free.*

GO OUT IN JOY

HIS BEAUTIFUL WORLD

The God who holds the whole world in His hands wraps himself in the
splendor of the sun's light and walks among the clouds.

Forbid that I should walk through Thy beautiful world with unseeing eyes:
Forbid that the lure of the market-place should ever entirely steal my heart
away from the love of the open acres and the green trees:
Forbid that under the low roof of workshop or office or study I should
ever forget Thy great overarching sky.

JOHN BAILLIE

Our Creator would never have made such lovely days, and given us the
deep hearts to enjoy them, above and beyond all thought, unless we were
meant to be immortal.

NATHANIEL HAWTHORNE

The whole earth is full of his glory.

ISAIAH 6:3 KJV

HIS BEAUTIFUL WORLD

The Word of God

For as the rain cometh down, and the snow from heaven, and returneth not thither, but watereth the earth, and maketh it bring forth and bud, that it may give seed to the sower, and bread to the eater: So shall my word be that goeth forth out of my mouth: it shall not return unto me void, but it shall accomplish that which I please, and it shall prosper in the thing whereto I sent it.

Isaiah 55:10–11 KJV

Not one word has failed of all His good promise.

1 Kings 8:56 NASB

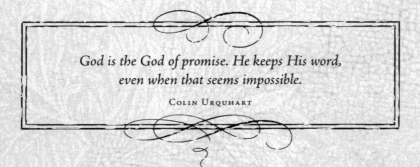

God is the God of promise. He keeps His word,
even when that seems impossible.

Colin Urquhart

THE WORD OF GOD

MADE FOR JOY

Our hearts were made for joy. Our hearts were made to enjoy the One who created them. Too deeply planted to be much affected by the ups and downs of life, this joy is a knowing and a being known by our Creator. He sets our hearts alight with radiant joy.

If one is joyful, it means that one is faithfully living for God, and that nothing else counts; and if one gives joy to others one is doing God's work. With joy without and joy within, all is well.

JANET ERSKINE STUART

Live for today but hold your hands open to tomorrow. Anticipate the future and its changes with joy. There is a seed of God's love in every event, every circumstance, every unpleasant situation in which you may find yourself.

BARBARA JOHNSON

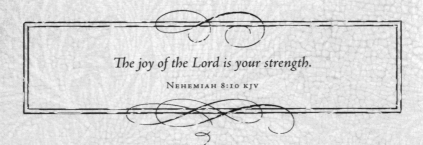

The joy of the Lord is your strength.

NEHEMIAH 8:10 KJV

MADE FOR JOY

GOD'S PEACE

Because of the tender mercy of our God, with which the Sunrise from on high will visit us, to shine upon those who sit in darkness…to guide our feet into the way of peace.

LUKE 1:78–79 NASB

Now in Christ Jesus you who formerly were far off have been brought near by the blood of Christ. For He Himself is our peace.

EPHESIANS 2:14 NASB

Grace, mercy and peace from God the Father and from Jesus Christ, the Father's Son, will be with us in truth and love.

2 JOHN 1:3 NIV

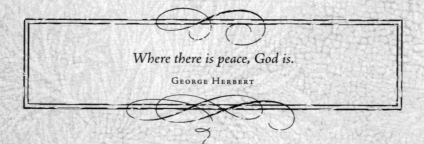

Where there is peace, God is.

GEORGE HERBERT

GOD'S PEACE

FOR HIMSELF

Although it be good to think upon the kindness of God, and to love Him and worship Him for it; yet it is far better to gaze upon the pure essence of Him and to love Him and worship Him for himself.

The reason for loving God is God himself, and the measure in which we should love Him is to love Him without measure.

BERNARD OF CLAIRVAUX

We desire many things, and God offers us only one thing. He can offer us only one thing—himself. He has nothing else to give. There is nothing else to give.

PETER KREEFT

The Lord alone shall be exalted.

ISAIAH 2:11 KJV

FOR HIMSELF

MY HELP

I will lift up mine eyes unto the hills, from whence cometh my help. My help cometh from the Lord, which made heaven and earth. He will not suffer thy foot to be moved: he that keepeth thee will not slumber. Behold, he that keepeth Israel shall neither slumber nor sleep. The Lord is thy keeper: the Lord is thy shade upon thy right hand. The sun shall not smite thee by day, nor the moon by night. The Lord shall preserve thee from all evil: he shall preserve thy soul. The Lord shall preserve thy going out and thy coming in from this time forth, and even for evermore.

PSALM 121:1–8 KJV

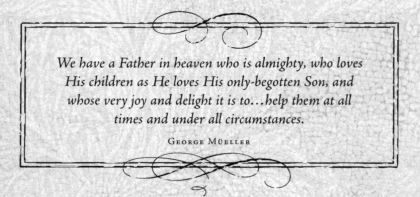

*We have a Father in heaven who is almighty, who loves
His children as He loves His only-begotten Son, and
whose very joy and delight it is to…help them at all
times and under all circumstances.*

GEORGE MÜELLER

MY HELP

....
....
....
....
....
....
....
....
....
....
....
....
....
....
....
....
....

NOTHING BUT GRACE

There is nothing but God's grace. We walk upon it; we breathe it;
we live and die by it; it makes the nails and axles of the universe.

ROBERT LOUIS STEVENSON

Grace is no stationary thing, it is ever becoming. It is flowing straight out of
God's heart. Grace does nothing but re-form and convey God. Grace makes
the soul conformable to the will of God. God, the ground of the soul, and
grace go together.

MEISTER ECKHART

Grace and gratitude belong together like heaven and earth. Grace evokes
gratitude like the voice an echo. Gratitude follows grace as thunder
follows lightning.

KARL BARTH

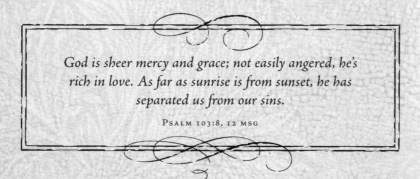

God is sheer mercy and grace; not easily angered, he's
rich in love. As far as sunrise is from sunset, he has
separated us from our sins.

PSALM 103:8, 12 MSG

NOTHING BUT GRACE

CONTENTMENT

I have learned to be content in whatever circumstances I am. I know how to get along with humble means, and I also know how to live in prosperity; in any and every circumstance I have learned the secret of being filled and going hungry, both of having abundance and suffering need. I can do all things through Him who strengthens me.

PHILIPPIANS 4:11–13 NASB

Be content with who you are, and don't put on airs. God's strong hand is on you; he'll promote you at the right time. Live carefree before God; he is most careful with you.

1 PETER 5:6–7 MSG

Godliness with contentment is great gain. For we brought nothing into the world, and we can take nothing out of it. But if we have food and clothing, we will be content with that.

1 TIMOTHY 6:6–8 NIV

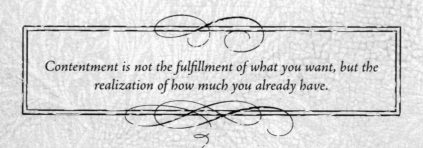

Contentment is not the fulfillment of what you want, but the realization of how much you already have.

CONTENTMENT

ALWAYS THERE

We need never shout across the spaces to an absent God. He is nearer than our own soul, closer than our most secret thoughts.

A. W. TOZER

God is always present in the temple of your heart…His home. And when you come in to meet Him there, you find that it is the one place of deep satisfaction where every longing is met.

Always be in a state of expectancy, and see that you leave room for God to come in as He likes.

OSWALD CHAMBERS

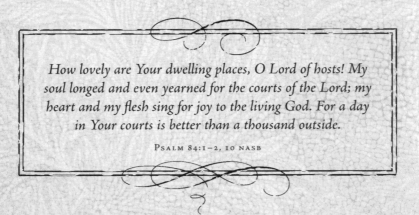

How lovely are Your dwelling places, O Lord of hosts! My soul longed and even yearned for the courts of the Lord; my heart and my flesh sing for joy to the living God. For a day in Your courts is better than a thousand outside.

PSALM 84:1–2, 10 NASB

ALWAYS THERE

FAITH

Now faith is being sure of what we hope for and certain of what we do not see. By faith we understand that the universe was formed at God's command, so that what is seen was not made out of what was visible. And without faith it is impossible to please God, because anyone who comes to him must believe that he exists and that he rewards those who earnestly seek him.

HEBREWS 11:1, 3, 6 NIV

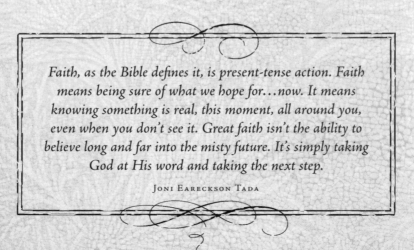

Faith, as the Bible defines it, is present-tense action. Faith means being sure of what we hope for...now. It means knowing something is real, this moment, all around you, even when you don't see it. Great faith isn't the ability to believe long and far into the misty future. It's simply taking God at His word and taking the next step.

JONI EARECKSON TADA

FAITH

ENDLESS WONDERS

Little drops of water,

Little grains of sand,

Make the mighty ocean

And the pleasant land.

Little deeds of kindness,

Little words of love,

Help to make earth happy

Like the heaven above.

JULIA FLETCHER CARNEY

As we grow in our capacities to see and enjoy the joys that God has placed in our lives, life becomes a glorious experience of discovering His endless wonders.

I will show wonders in the heavens and on the earth.

JOEL 2:28–30 NIV

ENDLESS WONDERS

JARS OF CLAY

But thanks be to God, who always leads us in triumphal procession in Christ and through us spreads everywhere the fragrance of the knowledge of him. For we are to God the aroma of Christ among those who are being saved and those who are perishing.

2 CORINTHIANS 2:14–15 NIV

For God, who said, "Let light shine out of darkness," made his light shine in our hearts to give us the light of the knowledge of the glory of God in the face of Christ. But we have this treasure in jars of clay to show that this all-surpassing power is from God and not from us.

2 CORINTHIANS 4:6–7 NIV

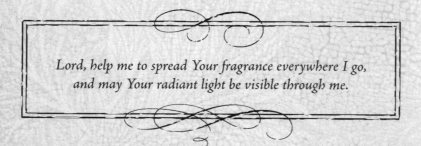

Lord, help me to spread Your fragrance everywhere I go, and may Your radiant light be visible through me.

JARS OF CLAY

JOY IS...

Joy is the touch of God's finger. The object of our longing is not the touch but the Toucher. This is true of all good things—they are all God's touch. Whatever we desire, we are really desiring God.

PETER KREEFT

Joy is really a road sign pointing us to God. Once we have found God... we no longer need to trouble ourselves so much about the quest for joy.

C. S. LEWIS

Joy is the echo of God's life within us.

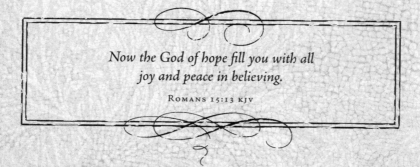

Now the God of hope fill you with all joy and peace in believing.

ROMANS 15:13 KJV

J O Y   I S . . .

FREE TO LIVE

God, your God, will cut away the thick calluses on your heart and your children's hearts, freeing you to love God, your God, with your whole heart and soul and live, really live.... And you will make a new start, listening obediently to God, keeping all his commandments that I'm commanding you today. God, your God, will outdo himself in making things go well for you.... Love God, your God. Walk in his ways. Keep his commandments, regulations, and rules so that you will live, really live, live exuberantly, blessed by God.... Love God, your God, listening obediently to him, firmly embracing him. Oh yes, he is life itself.

DEUTERONOMY 30:6–9, 16, 20 MSG

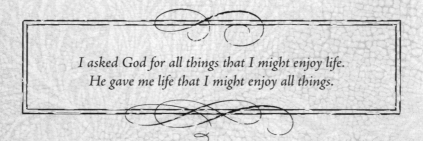

I asked God for all things that I might enjoy life.
He gave me life that I might enjoy all things.

FREE TO LIVE

SOMEONE SPECIAL

The Creator thinks enough of you to have sent Someone very special so that you might have life—abundantly, joyfully, completely, and victoriously.

When we love someone, we want to be with them, and we view their love for us with great honor even if they are not a person of great status. For this reason—and not because of our great status—God values our love. So much, in fact, that He suffered greatly on our behalf.

JOHN CHRYSOSTOM

One of Jesus' specialties is to make somebodies out of nobodies.

HENRIETTA MEARS

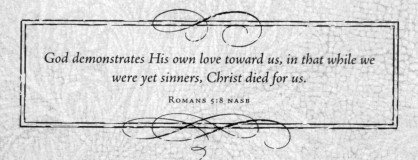

God demonstrates His own love toward us, in that while we were yet sinners, Christ died for us.

ROMANS 5:8 NASB

SOMEONE SPECIAL

The Garden of My Life

At that same time, a fine vineyard will appear. There's something to sing about! I, God, tend it. I keep it well-watered. I keep careful watch over it so that no one can damage it.... Even if it gives me thistles and thornbushes, I'll just pull them out and burn them up. Let that vine cling to me for safety, let it find a good and whole life with me, let it hold on for a good and whole life.

Isaiah 27:2–5 msg

Abide in Me, and I in you. As the branch cannot bear fruit of itself unless it abides in the vine, so neither can you unless you abide in Me. I am the vine, you are the branches; he who abides in Me and I in him, he bears much fruit, for apart from Me you can do nothing.

John 15:4–5 nasb

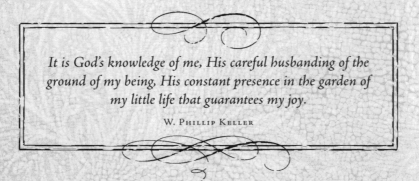

It is God's knowledge of me, His careful husbanding of the ground of my being, His constant presence in the garden of my little life that guarantees my joy.

W. Phillip Keller

THE GARDEN OF MY LIFE

SETTLED IN SOLITUDE

Solitude liberates us from entanglements by carving out a space from which we can see ourselves and our situation before the Audience of One. Solitude provides the private place where we can take our bearings and so make God our North Star.

OS GUINNESS

Settle yourself in solitude and you will come upon Him in yourself.

TERESA OF AVILA

We must drink deeply from the very Source the deep calm and peace of interior quietude and refreshment of God, allowing the pure water of divine grace to flow plentifully and unceasingly from the Source itself.

MOTHER TERESA

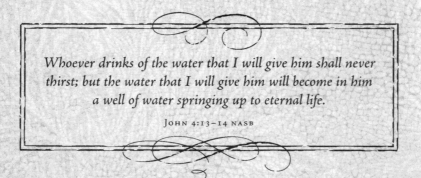

Whoever drinks of the water that I will give him shall never thirst; but the water that I will give him will become in him a well of water springing up to eternal life.

JOHN 4:13–14 NASB

SETTLED IN SOLITUDE

UNFAILING LOVE

Your love, O Lord, reaches to the heavens, your faithfulness to the skies. Your righteousness is like the mighty mountains, your justice like the great deep.... How priceless is your unfailing love! Both high and low among men find refuge in the shadow of your wings. They feast on the abundance of your house; you give them drink from your river of delights. For with you is the fountain of life; in your light we see light.

PSALM 36:5–9 NIV

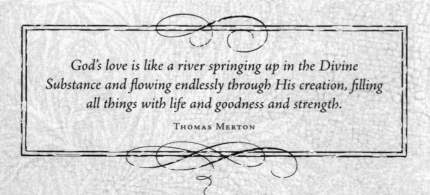

God's love is like a river springing up in the Divine Substance and flowing endlessly through His creation, filling all things with life and goodness and strength.

THOMAS MERTON

UNFAILING LOVE

DREAMS FULFILLED

Lift up your eyes. Your heavenly Father waits to bless you—in inconceivable ways to make your life what you never dreamed it could be.

ANNE ORTLUND

God created us with an overwhelming desire to soar.... He designed us to be tremendously productive and "to mount up with wings like eagles," realistically dreaming of what He can do with our potential.

CAROL KENT

The human heart, has hidden treasures,
In secret kept, in silence sealed;—
The thoughts, the hopes, the dreams, the pleasures,
Whose charms were broken if revealed.

CHARLOTTE BRONTË

I'll lead you to buried treasures, secret caches of valuables—
Confirmations that it is, in fact, I, God...who calls
you by your name.

ISAIAH 45:3 MSG

DREAMS FULFILLED

OF GREAT VALUE

Are not five sparrows sold for two pennies? Yet not one of them is forgotten by God. Indeed, the very hairs of your head are all numbered. Don't be afraid; you are worth more than many sparrows.

LUKE 12:6–7 NIV

For God bought you with a high price. So you must honor God with your body.

1 CORINTHIANS 6:20 NLT

For you know that it was not with perishable things such as silver or gold that you were redeemed…but with the precious blood of Christ, a lamb without blemish or defect.

1 PETER 1:18–19 NIV

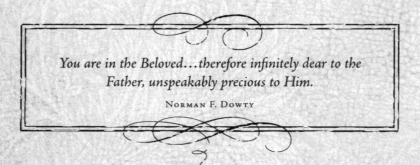

You are in the Beloved…therefore infinitely dear to the Father, unspeakably precious to Him.

NORMAN F. DOWTY

OF GREAT VALUE

NEW EVERY MORNING

Morning has broken like the first morning,

Blackbird has spoken like the first bird....

Praise with elation, praise every morning,

God's re-creation of the new day!

ELEANOR FARJEON

Always new. Always exciting. Always full of promise. The mornings of our

lives, each a personal daily miracle!

GLORIA GAITHER

That is God's call to us—simply to be people who are content to live close

to Him and to renew the kind of life in which the closeness is felt and

experienced.

THOMAS MERTON

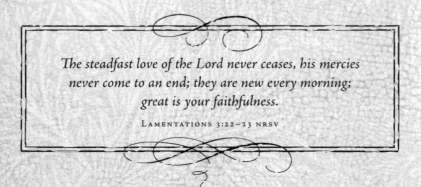

*The steadfast love of the Lord never ceases, his mercies
never come to an end; they are new every morning;
great is your faithfulness.*

LAMENTATIONS 3:22–23 NRSV

NEW EVERY MORNING

THE LORD'S PRAYER

Our Father which art in heaven, Hallowed be thy name. Thy kingdom come. Thy will be done in earth, as it is in heaven. Give us this day our daily bread. And forgive us our debts, as we forgive our debtors. And lead us not into temptation, but deliver us from evil: For thine is the kingdom, and the power, and the glory, for ever. Amen.

MATTHEW 6:9–13 KJV

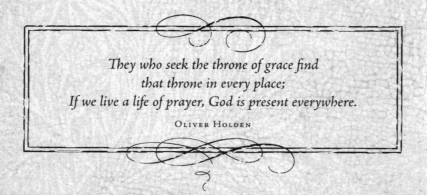

They who seek the throne of grace find
that throne in every place;
If we live a life of prayer, God is present everywhere.

OLIVER HOLDEN

THE LORD'S PRAYER

WATCHFUL CARE

He paints the lily of the field,

Perfumes each lily bell;

If He so loves the little flowers,

I know He loves me well.

MARIA STRAUS

God cares for the world He created, from the rising of a nation to the

falling of the sparrow. Everything in the world lies under the watchful gaze

of His providential eyes, from the numbering of the days of our life to the

numbering of the hairs on our head. When we look at the world from that

perspective, it produces within us a response of reverence.

KEN GIRE

God's in His heaven—

All's right with the world!

ROBERT BROWNING

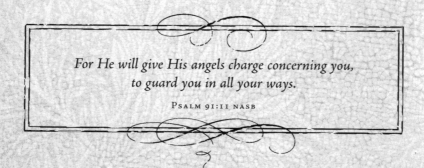

For He will give His angels charge concerning you,
to guard you in all your ways.

PSALM 91:11 NASB

WATCHFUL CARE

SONG OF PRAISE

"Behold, God is my salvation, I will trust and not be afraid; for the Lord
God is my strength and song, and He has become my salvation."
Therefore you will joyously draw water from the springs of salvation.

ISAIAH 12:2–3 NASB

The Lord is my strength and my song; he has become my salvation.
He is my God, and I will praise him, my father's God, and I will exalt
him…. Who is like you—majestic in holiness, awesome in glory,
working wonders?

EXODUS 15:2, 11 NIV

Then I heard something like the voice of a great multitude and like the
sound of many waters and like the sound of mighty peals of thunder,
saying, "Hallelujah! For the Lord our God, the Almighty, reigns.
Let us rejoice and be glad and give the glory to Him."

REVELATION 19:6–7 NASB

*Since God is Lord of heaven and earth,
how can I keep from singing?*

SONG OF PRAISE

BY LOVE ALONE

By love alone is God enjoyed; by love alone delighted in, by love alone approached and admired. His nature requires love.

THOMAS TRAHERNE

Love does not allow lovers
to belong anymore to themselves,
but they belong only to the Beloved.

DIONYSIUS

There is an essential connection between experiencing God, loving God, and trusting God. You will trust God only as much as you love Him, and you will love Him to the extent you have touched Him, rather than He has touched you.

BRENNAN MANNING

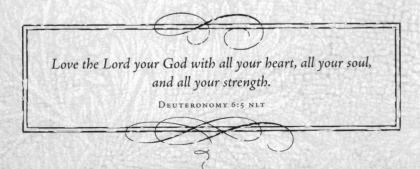

Love the Lord your God with all your heart, all your soul, and all your strength.

DEUTERONOMY 6:5 NLT

BY LOVE ALONE

SEEK THE LORD

The God who made the world and everything in it is the Lord of heaven and earth.... He himself gives all men life and breath and everything else.... God did this so that men would seek him and perhaps reach out for him and find him, though he is not far from each one of us. "For in him we live, and move, and have our being."

ACTS 17:24–28 NIV

I love those who love me; and those who diligently seek me will find me.

PROVERBS 8:17 NASB

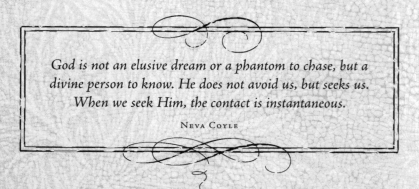

God is not an elusive dream or a phantom to chase, but a divine person to know. He does not avoid us, but seeks us. When we seek Him, the contact is instantaneous.

NEVA COYLE

SEEK THE LORD

DESTINY

Recognizing who we are in Christ and aligning our life with God's purpose for us gives a sense of destiny.... It gives form and direction to our life.

JEAN FLEMING

When we live life centered around what others like, feel, and say, we lose touch with our own identity. I am an eternal being, created by God. I am an individual with purpose. It's not what I get from life, but who I am, that makes the difference.

NEVA COYLE

God has a purpose for your life and no one else can take your place.

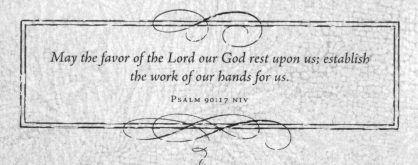

May the favor of the Lord our God rest upon us; establish the work of our hands for us.

PSALM 90:17 NIV

DESTINY

PATHS OF LIFE

But the path of the righteous is like the light of dawn, that shines brighter and brighter until the full day.

PROVERBS 4:18 NASB

You have made known to me the paths of life; you will fill me with joy in your presence.

ACTS 2:28 NIV

Thy word is a lamp unto my feet, and a light unto my path.

PSALM 119:105 KJV

Come, and let us go up to the mountain of the Lord…and he will teach us of his ways, and we will walk in his paths.

MICAH 4:2 KJV

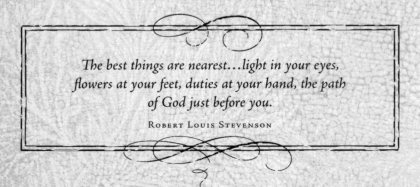

The best things are nearest…light in your eyes,
flowers at your feet, duties at your hand, the path
of God just before you.

ROBERT LOUIS STEVENSON

PATHS OF LIFE

GOD LISTENS

Open wide the windows of our spirits and fill us full of light; open wide the door of our hearts, that we may receive and entertain Thee with all our powers of adoration.

CHRISTINA ROSSETTI

We come this morning—
Like empty pitchers to a full fountain,
With no merits of our own,
O Lord—open up a window of heaven...
And listen this morning.

JAMES WELDON JOHNSON

God listens in compassion and love, just like we do when our children come to us. He delights in our presence.

RICHARD J. FOSTER

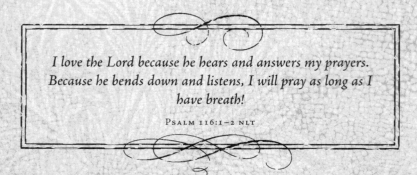

I love the Lord because he hears and answers my prayers. Because he bends down and listens, I will pray as long as I have breath!

PSALM 116:1–2 NLT

GOD LISTENS

Delight in the Lord

Delight yourself in the Lord and he will give you the desires of your heart. Commit your way to the Lord; trust in him and he will do this: He will make your righteousness shine like the dawn, the justice of your cause like the noonday sun.

PSALM 37:4–6 NIV

Send forth your light and your truth, let them guide me; let them bring me to your holy mountain, to the place where you dwell. Then will I go to the altar of God, to God, my joy and my delight.

PSALM 43:3–4 NIV

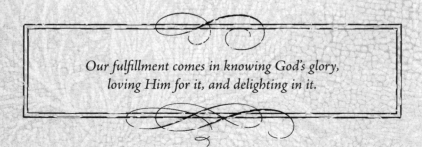

Our fulfillment comes in knowing God's glory,
loving Him for it, and delighting in it.

DELIGHT IN THE LORD

SHINING THROUGH

Don't ever let yourself get so busy that you miss those little but important extras in life—the beauty of a day…the smile of a friend…the serenity of a quiet moment alone. For it is often life's smallest pleasures and gentlest joys that make the biggest and most lasting difference.

Someone said to me once that we can see the features of God in a single smile. Look for that smile in the people you meet.

CHRISTOPHER DE VINCK

Dear Lord…shine through me, and be so in me that every soul I come in contact with may feel Your presence in my soul…. Let me thus praise You in the way You love best, by shining on those around me.

JOHN HENRY NEWMAN

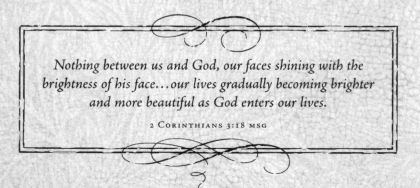

Nothing between us and God, our faces shining with the brightness of his face…our lives gradually becoming brighter and more beautiful as God enters our lives.

2 CORINTHIANS 3:18 MSG

SHINING THROUGH

HOLY AND WHOLE

May God himself, the God who makes everything holy and whole, make you holy and whole, put you together—spirit, soul, and body—and keep you fit for the coming of our Master, Jesus Christ. The One who called you is completely dependable.

1 THESSALONIANS 5:23–24 MSG

So spacious is he, so roomy, that everything of God finds its proper place in him without crowding. Not only that, but all the broken and dislocated pieces of the universe—people and things, animals and atoms—get properly fixed and fit together in vibrant harmonies.

COLOSSIANS 1:19–20 MSG

He has made everything beautiful in its time.

ECCLESIASTES 3:11 NIV

God's fingers can touch nothing but to mold it into loveliness.

GEORGE MacDONALD

HOLY AND WHOLE

TOTALLY AWARE

God is every moment totally aware of each one of us. Totally aware in intense concentration and love.... No one passes through any area of life, happy or tragic, without the attention of God with him.

EUGENIA PRICE

Because God is responsible for our welfare, we are told to cast all our care upon Him, for He cares for us. God says, "I'll take the burden—don't give it a thought—leave it to Me." God is keenly aware that we are dependent upon Him for life's necessities.

BILLY GRAHAM

You are God's created beauty and the focus of His affection and delight.

JANET L. WEAVER SMITH

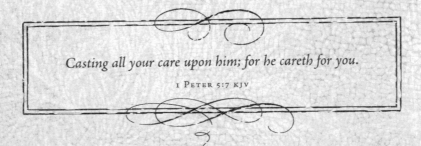

Casting all your care upon him; for he careth for you.

1 PETER 5:7 KJV